# The Truth About Broken

*The Unfixed Version of Self-love*

Hannah Blum

## THE TRUTH ABOUT BROKEN

**This book is dedicated to my parents, Danise and Mark Blum.**

*You are the reason I am who I am. You allowed me to blossom in my offbeat timeframe and to my own compass.*

**To my Uncle, Paul Blum**

*You define what it means to be strong, to be giving, to be loving, and especially what it means to be human. Your outlook on life is perhaps why I have learned to embrace the parts of myself labeled as flawed. I cherish every moment we have spent together. I learned from you, to look at life with a sense of humor.*

**The Truth About Broken**

*For those of you living with a mental illness. I see you. You are light and a gift to this world. This book is for you.*

*It is from our broken that we bloom.*

# Contents

# Introduction

In 2010 my path in life changed forever when I was involuntarily placed into a mental hospital at the age of 20 and diagnosed with bipolar 2 disorder. I went from Prom Queen to a mental patient in the blink of an eye. At the time, I thought it was the road to what I believed would be jagged and dark, but little did I know it was a journey toward a passionate life. A beginning toward finding my authentic self and loving all of that flawed person.

The experiences I have faced, the people I have met, the stories I have been gifted with have shaped my ideas and beliefs about living beautifully and authentically. It is in the parts of myself and my journey that are labeled as "broken" that I found my identity, beauty, purpose, and most importantly, it's where I found genuine self-love. Part of my purpose is to share these lessons through my writings. I am sharing the story and inspiration behind the quotes and poetry I have been keeping since I was a child up until now. I did not write this book as someone who has it all together, someone healed, or who has attained perfection or enlightenment. No, not at all.

In this book I hope to inspire you to embrace the *unfixed version* of yourself. I hope to empower each one of you to embrace what makes you different—because what makes you different is awesome. Each part of this book should be looked at as its own individual piece. I encourage you to take your time with each section. I will pose questions and prompts in various places throughout the book for you to free-write if you feel inclined to do so.

These are the parts of myself that over the last decade, into my late twenties, I have learned to accept, including the pain. I observe with compassion and listen with the intent to deepen my perception of the world around me. People only know and see the version of me that embraces what makes me different; what makes me broken. I have never shared my story on a personal level, sharing details that go beyond the surface, until now. It's time to share some of the stories of both myself and others who have inspired my words. Opening my journal and parts of my life to those of you reading.

The majority of this book focuses on my life with bipolar disorder; however, these experiences are relatable whether you live with a mental illness or not. The stories featured will give you a different perspective on people with a mental illness. It will also enlighten you on the severity of stigma and how it pertains to us all. This is a side of the story you don't hear or see in the media.

I do not want to fix or change you because you don't need to be fixed. I believe that empowerment doesn't come from fixing you, it comes from finding power in what you think needs to be fixed. I want you to love the person reading this line regardless of where you are in life.

*I don't want you to think, I want you to feel.*

This is the truth about *broken.*

# PART: Therapy Session #5

*Self-love is not attained; it's awakened.*

A couple of years ago I felt the need to go back to therapy. I had not been to therapy in a few years, which may surprise a lot of people, as I am a mental health advocate. However, what works for some people does not work for others. My journal and writing, since I was a child, has been the outlet where I feel free to express my emotions.

At this point, it had been about five years since the mental hospital. I felt stable, but then out of the blue I hit a low, then I went up and then quickly back down; then I self-harmed, felt like shit, and when I voiced this to my mom, she told me to go to therapy for her sanity.

I hesitated and fought back for a while but eventually surrendered when my mother spoke to me. The worry in her tone encouraged me to go back to therapy, so I did just to put her at ease—but I didn't get it. I was in the best physical shape, dating, reading self-help books, doing yoga, dieting and reflecting—but it was short term. There was still an emptiness within me that was holding me back. Who I had become wasn't clicking. Even though I was occasionally very happy, there was a part of me that just wasn't connecting to long term contentment.

When I told my psychiatrist, she agreed that it was time for me to go back to therapy, even if it were just for a few sessions. She also suggested that I switch from a female to a male therapist. Supposedly the male doctor she recommended possessed a calming and confident manner in dealing with people like me, and with individuals living with bipolar disorder. I thought to myself, "Oh great, I'm sure he's the Bipolar Wizard of Oz." I was dreading the appointment. I hated sitting there, getting bombarded with questions in hopes that I would break down. I said out loud as I pulled into the parking lot, "It won't happen."

If you are curious as to why I struggle with therapy I will give you a brief answer—I struggle with therapy because I am petrified that my words will be misconstrued, and I will be thrown back into a mental hospital, as I learned that lesson in 2010.

When I walked into the office, there he was, waiting for me, Dr. Mike. He was sitting with his legs crossed, wearing slippers, in a large comfortable looking chair. His glasses were perfectly placed on his calm and gentle face. Dr. Mike looks like a mixture between Steve Jobs and Dr. Mark Greene from the television series *ER*. He seemed incredibly sane, which made me think something was off about him.

I checked my watch to see if I was late, but I was five minutes early. The first session was a breeze—history, diagnosis, family, education, insurance, etc., and ended with my goals for therapy. I didn't have any.

Dr Mike is one of the more heavily sought-after therapists in the area, and after waiting three weeks for the initial assessment and first appointment, I was encouraged to make follow up appointments throughout the next four months. It was a slow process for me to feel comfortable with opening up to this man. I found him cocky, which later translated into him calling me out on my bullshit. Where I would occasionally catch him staring with what I imagined disapproval at my stiff posture, he would immediately lift my spirits with a compliment. I would retort with annoying smart-ass remarks, as I was thrown off. My defensive posture was locked and loaded. I looked at the clock and twiddled my thumbs like a five-year-old. We were getting nowhere, and I usually started every conversation with something similar to:

"I am really fine. Grateful for all that I have. Not sure why I am here, but really fine; I mean, do you see what's going on in other places in the world?"

However, Dr. Mike remained calm, asked me questions about my life, but didn't do any deep digging in the first couple of sessions; actually, no surprises in the first four sessions. I finally requested a longer session time for the remaining appointments. There was a need for me to have resolution when time was up! He then requested that I bring in ten photos of myself taken over the last 20 years of my life. There were no specific guidelines; I just had to be in them. He told me not to overanalyze the assignment; just pick ten photos and bring them in.

I didn't think about it, and minutes before I had to leave for the fifth session I jumped on Facebook, printed some photos, and grabbed some from various albums. I bolted out the door to the appointment.

I figured Dr. Mike was going to put me through the common therapeutic exercises that I had been through a million times-- *Hannah, what would you tell that girl in the picture?* And I would reply, *that she was beautiful!* (forced tears streaming down my face!). However, I was completely wrong in my assumptions about Dr. Mike.

In those first few sessions, where Dr. Mike remained quiet, he was observing me and gauging how he was going to approach me. He knew I was not going to be easy, so he analyzed every movement, every word, and every reaction. He didn't push me because he knew that if he did, I would never come back. He was right, I would not have returned.

He and I started having a casual conversation. At one point he asked me to take out the pictures and place them on the table. His tone didn't startle me or make me anxious about what was to come. I did as he asked and sat back in the chair.

Dr. Mike: "Hannah, what is your relationship like with yourself?"

I immediately tensed up.

Me: "Um, what do you mean? I am pretty confident. I mean, I have insecurities just like everyone else but really I'm fine with myself."

He remained silent.

The thing that Dr. Mike figured out about me that no one else could was that I didn't do well with silence. He knew questions

4

would only lead to fake answers—and the longer he remained silent, the more I would open up.

Me: "Well, I used to have problems with self-abuse and struggled with self-love but I think I'm better now. I guess it was rough battling myself and bipolar, but yeah. I don't know if that answered your question."

He leaned forward in his chair.

Dr. Mike: "I want you to take a couple of minutes and look at those pictures of yourself from the past."

I looked down at the pictures briefly, pretending to really analyze them, when I was in a daydream. I didn't know what to say and thought, "Yeah, those are pictures of me," would be sufficient.

He sat quietly and then looked up to me with serious yet empathetic eyes that almost made me want to cry.

Dr. Mike: "Look at the pictures again, except this time, I want you to answer this in your head first—What did you think of yourself when you first saw that picture? Because I know you remember."

I felt my stomach drop because he was right. I could remember exactly what I thought of myself. I could put myself back in the exact moment mentally and emotionally. *What did I think?* I hated myself in *every. single. one.* Each one had a story of disconnection. They ranged from the time I was a kid to age twenty-five. I looked up at Dr. Mike again, but his face was unemotional, which put me at ease. He knew that I was at my most vulnerable at that point.

Dr. Mike: "Hannah. What did you think about yourself in those pictures?"

I took a moment and looked around the room. I remember staring at a piece of art hanging on the wall of a woman and a man dancing in the middle of a street. She was wearing a red dress and the man wore a tux. The picture portrayed a wet street. It was evident that it was supposed to be a scene captured after it had been raining.

I looked back at Dr. Mike, and for the first time, I revealed the truth out loud.

Me: *"I hated myself in every single one."*

Dr. Mike: "Is that a coincidence?"

Me: "Well…" I paused and debated going further. I looked towards the clock, which was off. He had turned it off before I came in.

Me: "No. It's not a coincidence. Any picture would reveal the same thing."

Dr. Mike: "You mean you would feel the same way no matter the picture?"

I got defensive.

Me: "Isn't that what I just said?" Immediately I apologized and put my hand on my head. I shook my head yes. I was not emotional. I was honest.

Dr. Mike: "What do you see now Hannah when you look at those pictures?"

I looked down at every picture one at a time. One picture from my childhood in my mother's rose garden, a few from high school, one from Prom, some from college, including one that I realized was only a few days prior to my mental breakdown—in it, I am smiling from ear to ear in a beautiful spring dress with my friends. Others are of me in my early twenties, shortly after the mental hospital. Reminding me of the journey, these images told untruths.

Me: "Honestly, I am in shock." I pointed to one of the pictures. "This is me at 23. I remember when I saw this picture on Facebook. I had a meltdown because I thought I looked so fat and disgusting. I thought I didn't have my shit together at this age and such low self-esteem. It was after my diagnosis of bipolar disorder, and I was just so fucking confused stuck between accepting or rejecting it. Now I look at it and realize I was growing; I was so young but thought I had to be somewhere else in my life. I was underweight at this time, and literally, I don't remember seeing this picture like…"

I pointed to the picture of me as a child in my mother's rose garden.

Me: "I was just a kid, but so emotional. Even at this age I felt so different from everyone else, and I thought something was wrong with me. I would go into my mother's rose garden and just drift in my imagination." I smiled. "I was a cute kid."

I put my hand on my head. It was surreal. I did this for every picture over the next hour. At the end, I sat back and took a deep breath.

Dr. Mike: "Hannah, can I ask you a question now?"

I shook my head yes.

Mike: *"Have you ever loved yourself?"*

It is the question that I had been ignoring for as long as I can remember. The one that truly revealed the deep problem within me—my self-hate. My inability to see the beauty of me in the present. The self-abuse that left scars on my body. Although my life was coming together and I had accepted my diagnosis of bipolar disorder, there was still a part of me that was trying to fix myself. To be okay with where and who I was. To be okay with the fact that I did live with a mental illness and went public about it. The moment society came knocking on the door and told me I needed to be fixed, the girl who was okay with her broken disappeared.

I hated myself for not thinking and feeling like everyone else. I hated that I couldn't rid myself of the emotions that were always present, no matter what I did. I hated that I couldn't be who I truly was.

Dr. Mike repeated the question, "Hannah, have you ever loved yourself?"

I answered, "No."

He continued, "Why is that?"

Me: *"Because loving myself has always felt wrong."*

# PART: The Current of Life

*It's with broken wings that I learned to fly.*

My early childhood summers are still unforgettable. The family would head north on 95 to spend a few weeks hanging out with my grandparents and extended family on Cape Cod, MA. It's one of the most memorable parts of my childhood. I especially loved my grandparent's obsession with Provincetown. So on rainy light traffic days, Grampy and Nana would pack a few of us up and head south, then north to the tip.

The outer cape beaches are meticulously engineered and natural considering the harsh cape conditions. There was the one beach where parking was level with the sand and provided easy access for beach goers. Proud owner of a lifetime Park Service membership, Grampy would flash his worn and dulled laminated card at the always polite park ranger and slowly roll by all of the campers and open windowed cars and SUVs with tailgates down, coolers and beach chairs crowding the pavement. Stern and serious expressions controlled his handsome and dignified face until he would find his favorite space empty, and then orders flew.

We jumped out onto the hot pavement and guided the camper in until there was a miniscule crack between the back tires and the parking stop. My Nana would begin boiling the water for pasta while taking in the views of her beloved dunes and the privacy they provided. I was excited and just so thrilled to plant my feet into pristine warm sand. My brothers and I so hyper crazy, blindly headed to the water, but to me it wasn't a welcoming fun type of beach. The waves crashed down with anger and I yelled to my nana, "I think the ocean is screaming." I'm an exceptional swimmer—in a pool. Oh, in a pool I'm a winner, and I love to swim, but Provincetown introduced me to the power of Mother Nature over and over again. I respected her. I felt her chaos.

One particular day while navigating the beach, I came upon my grandfather chatting it up with a young guy in his early to mid-twenties. I was 12 years old at that time. I ran over and my grandfather introduced me to the handsome stranger, who at the time was in the Navy. His name was Jackson. It was no surprise my grandfather was in the heat of conversation, being that he, in his early twenties, had been in the Navy as well.

Before I joined my cousins heading into the water, my grandfather nodded his head towards me and asked Jackson, "Any advice for a new P-Town swimmer?" He looked out at the ocean and then back to me. His eyes were a deep brown, the type of eyes that drew you in.He knelt down on one knee and pointed toward the ocean, "You know what a current is?" I shook my head *no*. He looked deeply into my eyes similar to an adult when telling a child something extremely serious.

"If you ever get caught in a current, remember it's much stronger than you. If you fight against it and try to swim out of it, you will most likely drown. You have to swim with the current. That's how you survive." I nodded in agreement, but there was something about what he said that made me uneasy. It was almost as if he knew that at some point in my future I would get taken under by a current.

The words Jackson spoke that day would become more relevant in my life than I could have ever imagined. *Swim with the current;* endless exhaustion at times but the alternative cycles one back to fear and hopelessness. The riptide takes you out to the unknown. You are in its clutches; at the mercy of an unforgiving force. I know this only too well. My riptides show up out of nowhere, harmless and quiet appearing at family functions and when I'm alone. No red flags, no lifeguard. I have drifted with currents and I have fought back with a vengeance. I have been left in unfamiliar territory and found both peace and despair. I don't fight the current anymore, because Jackson was right—if I want to survive, I have to swim with the current of my life.

# PART: A Real Prom Queen

*There is no bigger bully than the one that exists inside my head; the one that hides behind my reflection.*

We watch TV shows that portray the "Prom Queen" as being the girl who has it all. She is pretty, popular and confident. Occasionally the Prom Queen is a mean girl but alas, the Prom Queen represents the girl who has her act together. If you look pretty, you feel pretty. If you are popular, you are secure. If you are Prom Queen, you don't end up in a mental hospital. Right? Yeah no.

My Prom Queen story differs from the one you've heard or seen portrayed because it's a real one.

It was Prom night and I was a senior in high school. I arrived back at the house a few hours before heading out with my face professionally made up and hair fabulously straight. I had been nominated for Prom Queen.

That afternoon my head was swimming and in no particular

direction. My mother defined these moments as dicey, when I insisted on silence regarding my activities. It was around junior year of high school that I started to display the symptoms of bipolar disorder; but it was a *teenage phase*, as one counselor put it, so I ignored it. We all dismissed the behavior. If I could explain to you what it felt like, I would put it like this—I was screaming in the middle of a crowded room, but no one could hear me. Not only could they not hear me, but on the outside, I appeared happy and perfect, which made my scream louder. It was like being trapped inside a different person begging to escape. Everyone walking around me waving and smiling because my pain was invisible to everyone outside of myself. I was alone fighting a war internally. This is the case for many of us who live with a mental illness.

I figured as I got closer to reaching the ideal, and the expectations everyone had for me, including myself, these problems would disappear. I believed my smile could contradict what I was feeling inside. Like many of us think, I just need to be ___ and all the pain and problems will disappear; because perfection, both in body and mind overshadows pain. Right? Really fucking wrong. It was never my dream to be Prom Queen, but when I was nominated it gave me a sense of relief; a delusional one.

All dressed up and ready to go, I went to head out the door where my friends were waiting, but made the mistake of checking myself in the mirror right before I left.

As soon as my eyes touched the mirror I was startled by my reflection. It was as if I was looking at a different person, someone separate from me. She appeared so put together, an image of myself like a snapshot which fails to reflect the self-doubt, self-loathing, and hatred.

The involuntary rush of rage that snapped me in half that night, that event, was the beginning of a long descent into darkness.

I had become so disconnected from myself that it was almost as if I were two people—the external and internal version of myself. One was a dream, the other a nightmare. It was the first moment that I recognized that something was not right—this was not a teenage phase; this was not normal. There was something going on inside that I had no control over.

Mascara ran down my face like a waterfall, black teardrops splashing against the floor. My eyes were dull and lost. My body began to shake with self-hate so intensely I thought I would physically break. I was immersed in total darkness not knowing up from down.

I fled to my room in a panic, my heart racing so fast I could hear it pounding in my head. I began frantically pulling the pins out of my hair. I stomped in my heels to the bedroom closet, grabbing all my awards over the years, photos, and anything that portrayed this ideal version of myself and threw them against the wall so hard that it left a hole—a hole carved out from my pain. The pain of feeling misunderstood. I lay on the cold hardwood floor in the remnants of my prom dress and slept for two days.

When it came time to go back to school, the following Monday, I persevered. It was a show, and I was the star of it. I wiped the dried mascara from my face and went back to school as if the prom was a huge success. I didn't know what was going on with me, but I felt I had no other choice but to continue. I got up, showered, fixed my hair, got dressed and drove to school as if nothing happened and made up some story that I recall made little sense. I was going to keep moving forward in the direction of attaining things to fulfill the emptiness inside of me, because again, Prom Queens don't go to mental hospitals.

Less than two years later I was walking into a mental hospital.

# PART: Finding Beauty in What We Fear

*Sometimes what we need is hidden in what we fear.*

I began self-harming when I was around thirteen years old. It was never with the intent of suicide, which is something many people get confused when they hear of people inflicting pain on themselves. In my situation, the end goal was to give an opening for my internal pain to escape from my body. You may call this delusional, and I used to think so as well, but the real delusion was feeling the need to hide my pain in fear of judgment.

I was fighting off so many storms—shame, extreme emotions, confusion, bipolar disorder, insecurities—all mixed into one pile of chaos. It was like trying to remain stable on shaking grounds while fighting off both a hurricane and a tornado. Self-harm was like popping a balloon with the intent of releasing the helium into the air. A way to free what existed on the inside. However, that liberation never occurred, and emphasized my self-hate. I felt the need to swallow my pain because the thought that I could be broken was more horrifying than the scars hidden on my body.

No one knew me because I didn't even know me, if that makes sense. I believed that creativity and imagination made a person weak, so I portrayed the complete opposite. I would roll my eyes when people would talk about art, when secretly I was listening with love. I voiced my disdain for anything that symbolized a more in-depth way of thinking. I feared that if I let people in even a little bit, they would see that I was an emotional being, they would eventually crack the whole case. My charm blinded people to the insecure person that existed within. Humor was a way for me to distract people, although it came very naturally to me, at one time it was a mask. Life became a stage for me to perform, and when the lights were on, I gave an Oscar-worthy performance. The only time I felt free was when I put pen to paper writing the words and stories that flooded my head daily.

My journal is the place where I learn about the parts of myself that are unseen—emotions, thoughts, insecurities, ideas and beliefs—I'm both the student and the teacher, visually engaging with my mind and trying to understand this part of me that feels impossible to comprehend. When I can visually see the invisible, I see pieces of strength, power and talent. My internal becomes tangible which makes me feel a sense of control. It doesn't reduce the pain or intensity of the emotions that surface, but I understand them now.

We fear what is unknown to us—*feeling* is one of those things, but acknowledging what we are hiding from reduces the fear we have of it.

Trust me, I have days that are so low that opening my eyes is painful. I am completely distant from myself and those around me. These deep highs and lows, insecurities will never change—but the way I perceive them can. Acknowledging their presence has changed those dark days into just days of my life instead of days defining my life, who I am, and my future. The insecurities, the highs and lows, are not something external, they are an essential part of who I am. It's the most powerful part of me—contributing to my success while also having the capacity to completely destroy me. The same goes for you, whether you live with a mental illness or not. Perseverance comes with understanding the issues you are working to overcome.

*Here is a story about becoming familiar with what is unknown.*

One night my niece refused to go to bed because she was afraid of darkness. So, I grabbed her hand and told her to come with me. I took her outside in the pitch black of the night. She was scared at first but after explaining to her the significance of this experience, she agreed to come with me. I also bribed her with candy and a trip to the Disney store, which is really what won her over. We went to the driveway and I told her to sit on the ground with me. She was frightened and I also felt some discomfort being in the dark of night. Then I told her to lay back on the ground. I did the same.

When we laid back, our eyes were immediately greeted and comforted by the stars in the sky. I heard the excitement in her voice as we looked at them. We told stories about what each star meant, how it got there—and for an hour we didn't move. As late as it was, she didn't want to go back inside to bed, she enjoyed the darkness.

I told my niece that the dark is part of our day that is just as important as when the sun is shining. It will always be a little scary and dangerous because we cannot see as clearly but when we sit in the dark our eyes slowly adjust. We can see the beauty in what we fear, the unknown. We see the stars.

She's slept with the lights off since then.

# PART: Down the Rabbit Hole

*Sometimes it feels like I am being suffocated by the surface of this world, and all I want to do is desperately escape.*

When I was in middle school, every day after school when the bus dropped me off, I would walk into my house, grab my headphones, my basketball and head outside. I would dribble it around my yard for hours until the sun went down, or I was forced to go inside. It didn't come off as odd to anyone because I was an athlete and everyone, including the neighbors, would commend me on practicing every day after school. For hours I would do this, and it got to the point that my hands started blistering from the basketball. I was dribbling just to drive attention away from what I was really doing, which was completely drifting off into my imagination. Down the rabbit hole into a place where I felt comfortable with who I was and was free from the pressure to be someone I was not.

I've been lost since I can remember. One of the most crucial elements to my success thus far is being able to drift off and get lost in my thoughts. I feel enclosed in my own little world. For hours I dance around like a little kid. Wearing earphones, jumping around until I'm exhausted. I take daydreaming to a new level but there is the physical component and the symbiotic relationship with my mind and body that is my rhythm and I own it. It's a sort of mind dance.

It also explains my obsession with *Alice in Wonderland*, a whimsical story by Lewis Carroll. Alice seemed to be her most authentic self when she was in "Wonderland." What we believe to be a sort of wonderland of madness is really a world of freedom. On the surface, Alice felt trapped; which is why she fell down the rabbit hole. This tale has always deeply resonated with me.

As a child, when I skipped out on playdates to isolate myself, or drifted through my mother's rose garden for hours, listening to music, I was lost and found at the same time. It continued into adulthood as well. It was where I could escape from the surface of this world, where I could jump down the rabbit hole to a place where being misunderstood was understood—where being emotional was beautiful—where being different was embraced. It was where I was me, and there has never been anything that felt freer than the moments where I felt I could be me. I didn't know who I was, and I know many of us don't know who we are, no matter what age and definitely not as a kid, but it was a different sort of lost—a disconnection. To this day I still get lost, but not with the intent to hide anymore.

# PART: My Best Friend Is Me

*If there is one thing I have learned it's that you cannot count on other people to save you from the edge, you have to learn how to save yourself.*

When I have been at my lowest, and when I was on the edge of life debating whether to jump, only one person could save me, and that person was *me*. I had to rebuild the friendship with myself, because the next time I am at the edge I may not be so lucky that my fall won't kill me. The person I trusted most needed to be me, and in order to build that bond I had to reestablish my identity. I had to become my own best friend.

The best tools we carry with us on a daily basis are our voice and our words—which if used properly can be the game changer in your relationship with yourself. You have to speak self-love and self-worth into existence. It's a conversation between your words and your thoughts. You have to speak to yourself like you would speak to your best friend.

Think about it; when your best friend feels like a total mess and opens up to you about their problems, and insecurities—you are most likely offering words of encouragement while being honest at the same time. I highly doubt you are screaming at them, "Yeah you are a mess and worthless!" You are probably telling them that although they are a mess right now that it's okay. You are exclaiming that they are so brilliant, talented and beautiful. If a guy or girl rejected them you go to battle for them, ripping the other person apart, unfollowing the rejector on social media, and making it clear that the other person is the one missing out on your friend.

When my friends feel like a wreck, I love suffocating them in love and more importantly in truth. They are blind to their beauty and we act as their honest and uplifting reflection. However, when it comes to us, we do the complete opposite. We are brutal. Why is it we feel we can only speak love to others and not to ourselves? Well, we can.

Once I asked my mother, "Is it weird that I talk to myself sometimes?" And my mother told me, "The best conversation you can have is the one you have with yourself." She's right.

Speaking out loud to myself is how I love myself even on the days I hate myself. I can't always control my thoughts and emotions, but I can control the way I speak to them, the way I speak to myself in those moments. Does it completely erase those negative thoughts, or cure my extreme emotions? No, but it balances the light with the dark. Some days my thoughts scream louder than my words, but I still speak it into existence even if it is just from my bed when I've been knocked off my ass by my emotions. It reminds me that I am still something even though I feel like nothing. It's the flicker of light within me when I am consumed in the dark.

I call it Delusional Confidence, and it's a method developed in the research lab of my own imagination. You literally speak to yourself as if you are having a conversation with your best friend. Now, do you do it at the dinner table with your family or at a party with your friends? No, please don't. You do it when you are alone with yourself, so you have complete freedom to be open. Turn your music up so loud that you can feel it in your body, and don't be afraid to be weird and out there---the best people always are.

Last night/morning I sat in the shower at 2 AM, and said to myself out loud "Hannah, you're fine, stop beating yourself down. You should probably go to bed earlier, maybe cut back on the cigs and take time for yourself, but okay so what? You're doing a great job, you're going to finish the book, stop thinking about your weight, you're beautiful, a mess, but a beautiful and kind mess, and that's okay. It's not about you. You're going to figure it out and this is going to be epic."

You don't need to Google affirmations, it's supposed to be all over the place because you are all over the place, and that is okay. It's what makes you brilliant. Although I call it delusional confidence, it's not delusional at all. Pain is a part of life, it's inevitable. Ignoring its presence is delusional, acknowledging it is sane.

The bottom line is, although there may be people who give you love and support, you are the person that needs you the most.

You are a beautiful and brilliant human being. I promise you that you are.

# PART: Follow in Your Own Footsteps

*Do not let others write the chapters of your memoir.*

It was flu season and people were rushing into the emergency room, pale, vomiting, hot and coughing. I was one of those people. Depending on the symptoms, some of us were placed in a private waiting room. There were only a few people in there. A woman, around the age of 90, intensely coughing into a handkerchief, sitting with her daughter who was frantically filling out forms.

Across from me sat a 15-year-old girl wearing athletic sweats. She had pale skin and long blonde hair tied in a tight ponytail. Her father was seated next to her with an ice pack in his hand. My throbbing head and glassy eyes rested on my mother's shoulder, void of emotion, observing everyone in the room. The old woman looked so ill and exhausted as she sat silently in her wheelchair with her eyes closed. I could sense her daughter's anxiety, as she kept bouncing her leg up and down, waiting to be called back. About 20 minutes into waiting I felt a different energy rising around me.

You know how you sense when someone's looking at you without seeing them directly?

The young girl sitting across from my mother and me kept looking towards me, then back to her father, whispering to him. I ignored it and closed my eyes. Then I heard, "Excuse me?" I opened my eyes. It was the father of the young girl, Missy. Immediately I sat up straight and smiled politely replying, "Yes?"

"Sorry to bother you, but my daughter is a little shy and wants me to ask, are you Hannah Blum?" She tugged her father's arm, clearly annoyed that he'd called her out for being shy.

The first thing I said to myself was, "You've got to be fucking kidding me?" I remember even laughing to myself about the ridiculousness of the situation. You have this dream that when a stranger recognizes you in public you are at your peak both emotionally and physically. However, that was not my circumstance at this moment. Missy had gotten a concussion after falling in her high school basketball game that night. She was a freshman at Brighton High School, which is the high school I attended. This public school was similar to a mini college—older and traditional—and resembled an old castle. While I was a student, the athletic department renovated a grand gymnasium that could compete with some colleges' athletic facilities. In the lobby of the gymnasium were glass cases from ceiling to floor that displayed the school's history dating back to the early days. Photographs, trophies, and newspaper clippings of students who were honored for their social, academic, and athletic achievements. The school was known for its sports and high society public events.

Missy and I didn't attend at the same time, but she knew who I was. In the glass cases, there were pictures of me as an athlete, my time on student council, on Prom, and Homecoming Court. It was a high school on steroids.

"My coaches and some of my teachers talk about you..." Missy continued, "I feel like I know you, kind of." Missy looked at me as if I was a celebrity and spoke to me with such respect and admiration.

Missy was extremely bright, kind, and ambitious. I asked her a lot about herself, which revealed that Missy and I were similar in many ways. We talked about school, sports, and her aspirations. I praised Missy on her accomplishments in school but told her not to put too much pressure on herself, that no matter what she did she would be just fine. I encouraged her to have fun and alluded to her that high school was not going to determine her path in life. As much as I wanted to spread a little wisdom, I didn't want to take away her enthusiasm. It was the last part of the conversation that has stuck with me to this day.

When the nurse gave me the signal that I would be called in shortly we began to say our goodbyes. It was right before I got up that Missy said the words I was hoping she wouldn't say. "I just want you to know that you are like my role model. I want to follow in your footsteps." It hit me like a dagger, but I had one moment to say something that I hoped would stay with her.

*"Follow in your own footsteps, Missy, because you are strong enough to do so."*

Hours later I would be involuntarily placed in a mental hospital. I didn't have the flu.

27

Your biggest role model is the person reading this line. Follow in your own footsteps. Be inspired by those who you admire, but don't define success based on attaining what they have. Missy thought I was full of life, when in reality I was empty of it. Little did Missy know that the person whose footsteps she wanted to follow was only a few steps away from a mental hospital. Follow in your own footsteps. Be your own role model.

We are born to build our own way in life, and as we grow, we develop and receive tools to do just that. However, that's not what happens. Although we have these tools in our possession, we are told how to use them. We feel the pressure to structure our lives in a way that goes according to the blueprint's others have laid out for us.

We worship celebrities and follow accounts on social media, comparing ourselves to strangers, believing that if we have what they have we will be fixed, and perfect. We feel this need to have some sort of guide who will help make life a little easier and less complicated. Instead of getting to know ourselves, we spend our energy on getting to know strangers whom we believe possess the magic potion for healing, happiness, and self-acceptance. It's supposed to prepare us, but in reality, it prevents us from building the strength we need to design our own path and define success and beauty according to our own beliefs. It's supposed to protect us, but it does the opposite—it prevents us from growing.

At one point in our life, the person we need help from is ourselves; and if you've lived a life where others have developed that strength for you or defined beauty, success and worth, you are left with nothing of your own. A lot of my quotes are based around the story of Missy and me, even almost a decade later. Writings about outside appearances and what the Universe was trying to teach me in that moment; I wanted Missy to know that she didn't have to be somebody in order to *be somebody*. Missy was not aspiring to be me at all—she wasn't aspiring to be a college drop-out, a mental patient, insecure with scars, and tainted from an eating disorder—but that's exactly who I was and where I was going at that time.

We look at people with assumptive eyes. We assume that they are living great lives. I value the stories, ideas and wisdom that people offer me based on their own experiences; but there is a difference between taking advice and trying to follow the lead of the person giving it.

What works for others may not work for you, because they are not you and you are not them. There is no way to see what lies ahead on our path in the hope that it will prepare us for the future. We build our path based on the obstacles that come about on our journey.

# PART: Be Wrong in the Right Way

*Do not judge my path in life simply because you do not understand it. You weren't born to walk this road; I was.*

When I went to the mental hospital the first thing they did was strip me of shoelaces, bra wires, hair ties, and drawstrings. My belongings were nowhere to be found. Even when I asked to use my Chapstick, they said no. As I undressed, I was slowly being stripped of my identity and molded into something else—*stigma*.

I wore baggy pants that slid off my hips and sagged. My hair was knotted in the back like a bird's nest. Lips chapped and cracked, eyes drawn and sedated. No bra, so my breasts hung, and my shoulders drooped over.

I will never forget the noise I heard when I walked through the doors to my unit—it was the sound of my loose sneakers clacking against the ice-cold floor. It was so loud at the time. *Clack, clack, clack,* as my feet dragged. It was similar to the sound you hear in a horror film when the victim is hiding from the insane psychotic killer, and all you hear is that slow, creepy noise which is the clacking of his shoes. That noise reminds of a time I felt like I should fear myself.

A few days into my hospitalization I was diagnosed with bipolar disorder. When the doctor told me that I had bipolar disorder, I immediately rejected it. I remember walking back to my bathroom and staring at myself in the mirror. I grabbed at my face and kept wiping my eyes. I was in disbelief that I had this disease that is portrayed in horror films. I couldn't see a girl that society labeled people with bipolar disorder to be—I didn't see a monster or some horrible individual. I saw a human, a daughter, sister, and a friend.

One thing living with a mental illness has taught me, which pertains to us all, is that our identity is so easily shaped by our environment. People with a mental illness are molded into stigma, which takes away their opportunity to create their own identity. It completely rips away the chance for us to love ourselves. You don't have to live with a mental illness to understand this truth. We create an identity around the beliefs, values, style, and appearance of others. It's the reason we struggle to love ourselves because we cannot identify with the person we are pretending to be. Our right to love ourselves is taken from us.

Our opinion of ourselves is based on the opinions other people have of us. If people believe X about people with bipolar disorder or any mental illness, then I must fit into that category because I have a diagnosis. I must be unlovable. I must be deranged. I must be an outcast. However, this is so far from the truth.

After opening up, I realized a lot about judgement and the people who judge us. I learned to value my truth more than I do other peoples' opinions.

When I receive messages like, "You have demons." "Women with bipolar are nut jobs and cheaters," "Mental illness isn't real," "People with bipolar disorder are monsters," they fail to make me insecure. Why? It goes hand in hand with one of my favorite sayings,

"If it doesn't apply, let it fly."

It doesn't affect me because I am none of those things. I know mental illness is real. I am not a monster. I am not a nut job. Insanity is taking the time out of your day to write a person a message such as the ones I shared with you. I am lovable, honest, caring, and capable. So are you.

Caring about what other people think of you is a one-way ticket backwards. When I decided to open up about bipolar and pursue a career in writing, someone very close to me, whose opinion I mistakenly valued at one time, told me it was the worst decision I could make. He would be right—only if I believed *him* over believing in *it*.

*It* referring to my aspirations, and *him* referring to the ignorant toxin preventing me from following my passion. Well, I believed in *it* over *him*.

When someone belittles us or makes us feel insecure, we don't question the other person, we question ourselves. *Their burden becomes our burden. Their beliefs become our beliefs.*

Always remember—Judgement is another word for fear. If those who judge you are unwilling to listen and understand, why do you have to be so willing to accept their ruling of you? It's important to think about it.

Whom do you aim to please or seek approval from?

What are you afraid you are being judged for?

Are you waiting for your dad to tell you he's proud of you? Are you waiting for your parents to finally accept your mental illness? Do you fear opening up because you are afraid others will judge you?

They will judge you, because no matter what we do in life, we will always be judged. So, we have to let go of seeking others' approval and acceptance. Waiting for someone to think you are great is preventing you from being great.

We strive to please others in hopes that we will hear three of the most powerful statements in the Universe.

*"I love you," "I'm proud," "I accept you."*

Hearing this, especially from those closest to us is the difference between thinking we are worthy and thinking we are pieces of shit going nowhere in life. However, we should feel loved by others in both high and low times. Even when we are going against the grain, we should still feel accepted. *Loyalty* and *love* are close friends. I was awakened to this when I was at the mental hospital.

Once a week, from 12-1 PM, family visitation hour arrived with anticipation. I didn't expect any of my family, including my parents, to come out as it was a long drive and they all had full-time jobs. Then I got a beautiful surprise one day. When I walked into the common area, I caught my brothers' huge heads peeking through a little circular window. My father, two brothers and sister-in-law came to see me. They each took turns coming in, and although it was short, I loved every second of it.

Even in a mental hospital at my lowest point, I remember that day hearing, *"I love you."* Their beliefs about life, mental illness, right vs. wrong, came second to the person they loved, *me.* It didn't matter that I was in a mental hospital. It did not matter that I had a diagnosis of bipolar, I was a person, a person they loved.

You deserve to hear those same words. You deserve to be surrounded by people who love you just as you are. There are people who will not make us question everything about ourselves. Unfortunately, these people may not be your parents or family, and this breaks my heart. I can't imagine how difficult it must be when you are rejected by close family members such as your parents. It can't be easy to let go of, but it's absolutely necessary.

You are not bad. Let me repeat, YOU ARE NOT BAD. We get so caught up in this belief that we do not deserve to be admired, respected, cared for, or loved. We are always giving as if we are compensating for being who we are. We invite hate into our lives by getting into friendships or relationships that make us feel insecure. We only hear the comments that make us feel bad. We reject the positive things people tell us. We are closed off to love and acceptance because we think we are undeserving of it. Let these thoughts go. Let go of the people who enhance these thoughts.

Take out a sheet of paper and answer these questions: Who makes you feel judged? Who makes you feel insecure? Why do you keep them in your life?

On a different sheet of paper answer these questions: Who are the people that bring joy to your life? What makes you smile? What are some of the positive things people have said about you?

Look at both sheets of paper. Take a moment. Then take that first sheet of paper, tear it up, and throw it the fuck away. Take the second sheet of paper and tape it to your mirror. That sheet of paper is the truth about who you are.

We have no control over the opinions of others, but we do have control over the opinion we have of ourselves. Stop defending yourself to people who have no right to judge you in the first place, and trying to prove to others that you are worthy. I will tell you. You are worthy. Say it out loud. Write it down fifty times in your journal and start believing that you deserve to live an awesome life.

If you are kind to others, then you are doing more than most. Those who are unwilling to accept you choose to live their life according to their beliefs, but that in no way requires you to do the same. Society is not yet accustomed to being okay with different, and they use it to their advantage, however, we don't have to let it put us at a disadvantage.

We will always be wrong in the eyes of some people. So if we are going to be wrong no matter who we are, what we do, what we have or whom we love, then why not be wrong for being honest?

Instead of being right, let's be *wrong* in the right way.

# PART: Happiness, Where Are You?

*The truth is—the more popular you are, the more alone you feel. The more you strive for perfection, the more dissatisfied you are with yourself. It's when we stop trying to attain happiness that we can feel it within us.*

**This is Tracy's story, I call it:** *Horny for Happiness*

Tracy entered the common room at the mental hospital dressed in a Chanel sweat suit with matching slippers. She was a new patient. Her blonde hair was perfectly cut in a fashionable long bob. However, the glitter of her appearance could not cover her swollen eyes and bewildered face as she entered the room.

During group therapy, the counselors would introduce themselves, then all of the patients would do so as well. About five minutes after a new patient entered, the counselor wasted no time, gently asking the newbie, "Why are you here?" I always thought to myself what a dumb question to ask right when a person walks in—"Oh, because this mental hospital got great reviews on TripAdvisor!"

Tracy sat there for about ten minutes, repeating the same thing over and over again, "I don't know why I'm here!" Each time she got louder and angrier. At one point her attitude got the best of her when she looked to all of us and said, "I don't belong with you people, you're nuts!" I thought to myself, "Who does she think she is?" I couldn't keep quiet.

"You are sitting here just like all of us, which makes you insane too. I mean, you're freaking wearing Chanel slippers at a mental hospital!"

The counselor waved frantically to me. I knew I would get in trouble, but I didn't care. Similar to Tracy, I was lucky enough to come from an upper-class family. Still, even at my lowest, I never felt entitled. It didn't give her a free pass either to use her wealth as a tool to make others feel like shit. I knew how most of the people sitting there could barely put food on the table at home. I hated Tracy at that moment for increasing the shame that was already so heavily weighing on all of us.

There was tension in the room. Tracy yelled at me, "You have no clue, you're a kid! What the hell do you know about life?"

I replied calmly, "Then enlighten me, Tracy. Enlighten me about life."

Tracy remained silent and turned her head with her nose high in the air and arms crossed tightly. Something was brewing. You could feel it. All of the patients watched as if it were a movie.

Tracy rapidly uncrossed her arms and turned towards me with

rage, "You don't get it!" She stumbled, "You're just...you belong here, not me!" Tracy looked like she was on the brink of finally releasing everything trapped within her. She was beginning to unravel.

The counselor who was only a couple years older than me at the time didn't know what to do. She moved her hands to quiet us both, "No one here is insane, ladies we..."

I cut the counselor off and yelled to Tracy,

"THEN WHY THE FUCK ARE YOU HERE TRACY?" The answer was very far from what I or any of us expected.

Tracy bolted out of her seat, stood on the couch and started screaming at the top of her lungs,

"I'M HORNY! I'M FUCKING HORNY! IS THAT WHAT YOU WANT TO HEAR? THAT'S RIGHT, I'M INSANE BECAUSE MY HUSBAND HASN'T FUCKED ME IN OVER A YEAR! IS THAT A GOOD ENOUGH ANSWER?"

Yup. Word for word.

The room went completely silent. The counselor put her hand over her mouth. Tracy stood there in her little Chanel slippers breathing heavily with her mouth parted in shock at what she'd just revealed to a room filled with strangers. I looked at Tracy with my mouth to the floor. No one knew what to do.

Then Ralph, a 50-year-old patient diagnosed with bipolar who had a killer sense of humor, broke the silence in the most epic way.

He slow-clapped. He did the freaking slow clap.

Then his buddy joined in. Eventually, we were all standing and giving Tracy a standing ovation for revealing that she was obviously very horny. Tracy started to laugh, and with tears falling down her face, she took a bow.

After that group session, Tracy let her guard down and took off the mask. Although we weren't friends at first, Tracy and I became close shortly after her performance. The Tracy that walked into that mental hospital had disappeared. We became friends, and I learned a lot about life during our time together.

Tracy was brilliant; attended an Ivy League school and cruised with ease throughout her academic career. From a wealthy background, she was a beautifully groomed woman in her mid-thirties. However, from the time Tracy was a teenager, she struggled with depression, anxiety, bulimia, and anorexia. It was evident in her appearance—extremely frail, pale, weighing no more than 120 pounds. If I could describe her look in one word it would be *empty*. Ironically, on the outside, her life was nowhere near empty.

Tracy had married in her early twenties resulting in a divorce only a few years later. The community that previously praised and loved her, suddenly wrote her off. She was alone, until she met Fred. Fred was a much older man who was well known and rich. When Tracy met him, she was at her lowest and more insecure than ever, but she ignored her problems, believing that more money, more things, a man— these would be the solution to her problems. Short term gratification was exactly that, *short*. As Tracy referred to it, "a short term high."

Fred built Tracy's dream home, she traveled all over the world and had everything money could provide. She was beautiful, well off and...happy. Although the outside looked perfect, everything on the inside was decaying. Fred's stepchildren despised her and referred to her as a "hungry gold digger," which increased her anxiety and mental health problems. She felt pathetic and Fred felt helpless in the situation.

Tracy revealed to us that Fred once told her, "Tracy, with gold comes some dirt, what can I tell you?"

She laughed, "I don't even know what the fuck that means."

Fred would take things from her in the hope that it would teach her a lesson or get her to snap out of it. She was like a child. Tracy found hope in prescription pills and wine…lots of wine and pills, to the extent that she overdosed, which is why she was with us.

She later told us that her actions were intentional. She was trying to commit suicide.

Obviously, the lack of sex was not really the reason she was there, but Tracy revealed that her husband didn't touch her with love at all. He hadn't in years. Fred wasn't a horrible person, he was old-school, conservative, and viewed life from an unemotional perspective.

She wanted a kid, but Fred refused to even discuss having another child and got a vasectomy. He was older and more settled in his life, and Tracy was more of a nuisance than a wife. She was in a constant battle with herself, everyone around her, and even the food put on her plate.

Tracy's story is similar to so many of us. The way we try to fill the emptiness within us with material things and ideals. Women who appear as though they are living the dream, but in reality, they are living in their own internal nightmare. Her story is relatable to anyone who is constantly trying to attain one thing after another in the hope that it will finally give them happiness, self-love, and love all around, but that day of fulfillment never comes. Over time, the collection of things and superficial beliefs only result in pure misery with an expensive price tag.

The more plastic surgery, the more weight lost, the more money gained, and status raised only brought Tracy to the conclusion that she was withering away inside, completely numb to everything and everyone around her. Even though she was surrounded by people, she was alone. People loved the image she presented more than they loved the person she genuinely was. Tracy told us that her closest friend in the world was their housekeeper, Margaret, who had been with them for years.

Tracy told me, "She's the only person that knows me, and loves me for who I am." It was Margaret who found Tracy after she overdosed.

However, as the days passed at the hospital, there was a sense of relief that came over Tracy, similar to my experience. She was forced to reveal everything about herself—her problems—and put it on the table. It was either going to work or not work, but she made it clear that she could no longer live a lie. She spoke with a sense of happiness and believed that change was possible in her life. It was at the mental hospital that she felt more like herself than ever. Tracy was desperate for self-love; she was horny for happiness.

A couple of nights before I was released, Tracy and I were chatting in the common area. She commended me on my ability to creatively use words to describe people and their circumstances. I was flattered. Tracy asked me to describe what I had learned from her experience in one sentence—she called it "her slogan"—so I did, and she loved every word of it.

*Chanel won't save you from the edge, she'll just make your fall look a lot more glamorous than the rest of us, but we all hit bottom just the same, with or without diamonds.*

At one time I thought happiness and confidence would come with conforming. If I can mold myself into what society has taught me that "happiness" looks like, then it's impossible for me to struggle. If I follow through on my plans, life will be perfect. If I hide my diagnosis of bipolar, it will eventually disappear. If I get married, then I will feel loved and worthy. If I maintain the perfect body, then I will feel confident.

We have this idea that if we attain X, if we achieve Y, if we get # of followers on social media, if we make this $$$ amount of money, and marry by a certain age, we will be happy. All of our problems and insecurities will disappear. It will bring us to the moment we take a deep breath and say, "I am happy, confident, and content." We have accumulated what we believed growing up equated to a good life. It's when that feeling doesn't come that the truth sinks in, and the truth is, we are lost.

The only time these things or beliefs satisfy us is before we have them in our possession, when they carry hope for a better life, but they don't. Trust me, I can tell you from experience, they don't work.

When I first entered the mental hospital there were three words I kept repeating over and over again. *It didn't work.* All the things that were supposed to make me happy, *it didn't work.* All the things that were supposed to make me feel beautiful only made me despise my reflection even more.

When you open yourself up, you allow so much beauty to come into your life. You start to attract people who are just like you, who understand you and love you for who you are. You are opening yourself up to opportunity and an awesome life with incredible people. You have to let these people in. They are your tribe, your community and your peers.

Exposing our broken, our truth, and embracing what makes us different is the gateway to being happy with who you are.

# PART: Lessons by Van Gogh

*An empty canvas leaves room for exploration.*

According to many historical experts, the artist Van Gogh lived with mental illness, specifically bipolar disorder. He suffered from his emotional extremes all the way up to his death. His pain is tragic, but out of his expression of these emotions and life experiences, he created incredible pieces of art. One of those pieces is *Starry Night* which I am sure many of you have seen or heard of. If you have not, look it up, because it's absolutely magnificent. A part that you do not hear about this specific painting, which is considered his most famous, is where it's inspiration began.

The answer is—in a room in a mental asylum.

In 1889 Van Gogh wrote a series of letters to his brother Theo during his stay at the asylum of Saint-Paul-de-Mausole where he was being treated for mental illness. In one specific letter, he talks about the inspiration for *Starry Night*, based on what he sees from his window.

> *Through the iron-barred window I can see an*
> *enclosed square of wheat...above which, in the*
> *morning, I watch the sun rise in all its glory...I*
> *don't know anything with certainty but seeing*
> *the stars makes me dream.*

The pain he was enduring emotionally is heartbreaking. He was struggling in a time when proper treatment for mental illness was non-existent. This caused his mental state to deteriorate, leading to his death. But the question is, why is that Van Gogh created his most famous piece at a psychiatric ward?

When you hit such a deep low, you are consumed by the rawness of your emotions, and the only part of life you can connect to, the only thing you can feel, is what is real. Van Gogh was present in what he saw outside his window, which gave him a very real perspective that was true to him and how he was feeling.

In his letter, Van Gogh speaks in what appears to be an uplifting tone. He speaks of what existed on the outside, which related to what was real— dreams and nature. the wheat, the sun, the stars.

The reason I really connected with this specific part of Van Gogh's story is because when I was at my lowest, scared and uncertain as I was, I was also empty of everything that once prevented me from seeing the world in its raw state.

At the mental hospital, we would get thirty minutes to go outdoors. It was nothing special, just a small area in the back of the hospital, but the first time I went outside, I was captured by the world I saw in front of me. It looked new.

There was nothing but an old wooden fence, a raggedy picnic table, and patches of grass. It was magnificent in its own vulnerable way. I could feel the humidity pressing against me, the grass had never been greener, and the sky was so blue. How could I have missed this?

I was free from trying to attain anything else outside of what was right in front of me.

Years before the mental hospital, when there were plans in place and standards to reach, I always pictured what my life was going to look like. Who I was in the present was never good enough. Never. I always needed to be more—to reach my potential, or the potential everyone else believed of me. Every time I attained one thing, I would feel the pressure to achieve something better; paint a picture based on what I believed others wanted or expected to see.

I was twenty years old when I walked out of the mental hospital—a college dropout, no job, no money, a runaway who was heading back to the place she ran away from—leaving with a diagnosis of something so foreign to me, bipolar disorder, or at least I thought so at the time. If you are thinking that this was the moment, I had some sort of enlightenment, it was not. However, I did see the world differently.

I walked out of the mental hospital with plastic bags filled with my belongings and waiting for my father to bring the car around. As terrified as I was, I felt calm. My truth was finally exposed, and surprisingly, it was a relief.

On the car drive home, I looked out to the silent country roads ahead surrounded by farmland and tobacco fields. Everything that was once dull was vibrant. For the first time I was present in what existed outside my window, and it was beautiful. My own version of *Starry Night*.

# PART: The Best You Is the Present You

*If you feel low or broken down, it's not the worst of you. It's the human in you.*

The *best you* is always the *present you*. We are prone to believe the opposite, which I did for far too long. I realized that in order to truly love myself I had to love myself in my own mess, not when I was completely cleaned up.

When people are constantly reminding us that we have the power to become a better version of ourselves, how can we love ourselves in the present? "Be your best self" only reinforces the idea that the person you are right now isn't good enough.

I am swarmed with tools, methods, and products that will help me overpower the emotions that have been present in me since I was a child. In the past, I judged my extreme emotions as weak and illogical, but that only intensified my emotional extremes by adding shame and guilt to the mix. Not only was I feeling, but thinking about how I was feeling, searching for ways to think about how I was feeling, working on methods to change the way I think about thinking about my emotions…yeah, too much right? Exactly. It is too much.

If we smile and meditate, we will no longer be depressed. If we change our mindset and spend $5,000 on a retreat, we will finally find happiness and have a problem-free life. Our social media feeds are filled with people telling us that we can live a better life, which, for some reason always equates to having a lot of money. However, these same people are telling you that happiness cannot be bought. Wait, what? It's the type of propaganda that inspires you to be someone better than the current version of yourself.

There is nothing wrong with making a lot of money posting inspirational content that is true to your beliefs. I strive to have a career doing the same thing, but there is a difference between inspiring and profiting off people's struggles. It's important to acknowledge this because it's part of the reason people can't embrace the raw version of themselves. We don't awaken people; we awaken them to the fact that they aren't living a good enough life. I call these people who preach about mental health and how we can "choose" to be happy, "inspirational drug dealers," because that's exactly what they are. Individuals who increase shame and call it "wellness."

People who are real and raw are the individuals who deserve the platform they stand on. People who don't pretend to know or have everything together, these are the people who have mastered the art of being human. You cannot embrace your broken if you are surrounding yourself with noise that is telling you to be fixed.

Self-help books have helped me grow in the most beautiful ways. I carry these books with me wherever I go, highlighting different parts and journaling about them. Exercise and taking time to reflect helps me connect my mind and body. I feel better when I am in good shape. Learning to let go and trust the Universe brought me closer to myself. These tools have helped me to grow and succeed. They are incredible and amazing. There are many people out there sharing their wisdom and methods about mindfulness that I think are brilliant. However, have these practices cured me of my mental illness? No. Have they erased all my insecurities and rid me of experiencing pain? No. Are these going to fix us? No, because we don't need to be fixed.

We are not entitled to a pain-free life, but we act like we are.

We feel the need to rid ourselves of every insecurity, characteristic, and emotion that doesn't fit into the sanity box. This exposure to mental marketing sets us up for failure and disappointment. We are begging for someone to tell us how to love ourselves, and how to embrace who we are.

Our emotions are constantly on trial, making us question every feeling and thought. Labeling emotions—sadness, fear, confusion, worry—and defining them makes us feel the need to rid ourselves of them. If we do not feel; we do not exist. Constantly being in a state of clarity is the equivalent to believing that it's never going to rain or storm again. Sunny days are here forever if you do $X$ or practice $y$. It's short term gratification that makes people like me, who are filled with emotions, feel like shit.

We fight our emotions and frantically try to swim out of them. We try to overcome our emotions without acknowledging them first. It's human nature to reject what we do not understand, but when it comes to the internal, ignoring what exists just prolongs pain. We refuse to acknowledge the truth about who we are so that we can fit this ideal that we believe will make us *happy, normal, worthy* and *successful.*

In my world, to not think or feel is to not breathe. When I resented my emotions, I began to resent myself. I thought if I portrayed the opposite on the outside, then my emotions would surrender. However, the harder I fought them, the more I was gasping for air.

The answer to loving yourself is learning to love the parts of yourself that you are desperately trying to fix. The trial is over, and the only crime you are guilty of committing is being your version of human.

We are not required to be healed to love ourselves. We do not have to attain what we believe is our "best self" in order to embrace who we are. Our best self exists in the present. Sure, there are always areas we can work on. I shouldn't smoke cigarettes, work so late and could ease up on some bad habits, however that doesn't mean I have to hate myself. I have the right to love myself, and so do you.

It seems logical to think our best self exists when we are completely put together—body, mindset, and financial stability—with no bad habits, completely centered and all our insecurities have disappeared. Who we *should* be is always better than who we are right now. The question is—who should you be? How do you know that the person you should be is better than the person you are?

I used to beat myself up with this word, *should.* I should have stayed. I should be someone better. It was only in the last couple of years that I acknowledged my inability to love myself in the present. I was never good enough as who I was—I could be better, smarter, skinnier, more successful, at a better place in my life and there was never a moment of peace where I was not trying to attain something else to make me a better person. It prevented me from living and increased my self-hate; which lead to more binging, purging and self-harm. However, we learn a lot on this journey if we are open to the experience of it instead of creating it in our head. The *should* creates unnecessary problems in our lives.

Becoming the person, we believe we should be is not a guarantee of happiness or success, but we treat it like it is. If there were certain criteria for living your best life—such as money, popularity, fame, and beauty—then why is it that so many people who have all of that are unhappy?

At one point in my life I realized that I was focusing all my energy on a person that didn't exist, the *should* version of myself, versus putting energy into the person I am, the one that is living, and breathing. Once I let go of the *should* and started looking at my mistakes and missed opportunities as lessons, life became a lot more enjoyable. That's not to say I still don't smack my head with the "I should have done" but in the big scheme of things I have learned it's what I do from here on that matters.

# PART: Getting Comfortable in Uncomfortable

*They are only our flaws if we allow them to be.*

The first time I opened up about my life with bipolar disorder was on a stage in front of a decent sized audience. It was never my intent to come forward about mental illness or to advocate. I definitely didn't see myself standing on a stage one day speaking about it.

Two months before that, I started volunteering in the mental health community. It had been years after being released from the mental hospital. I went back to college, had a job as a nanny, and life seemed to be "normal." It seemed as though hiding my diagnosis was the right thing to do. However, there was still something inside of me that needed to know more about my mental illness and the people who had it. It was a part of me that I was pretending was not there. This was when I decided to volunteer.

One organization needed ongoing help in the front office. It was a non-profit organization that provided mental health services and resources. I went once a week for two hours doing little jobs around the office. When they asked what the motivation was behind volunteering, I told them that my sister was diagnosed with bipolar. I don't have a sister. I was in no way ready to open up to anyone. However, I could tell they were curious, especially after I slipped in the middle of a conversation with the employees about sibling rivalries. I chimed in about how I grew up with older brothers who used to be at each other's throat when they were teenagers. Someone even remarked, "Didn't you have a sister?" I immediately replied, "Oh yeah, well, um yeah, I think of my sister as my brother, I guess." *Yeah, that was an awkward moment.*

A couple of weeks into volunteering, an employee asked me if I could help organize her office. Her name was Ally. Ally was a gentle soul who was hard-working and compassionate. She had dark brown hair cut to her shoulders, green eyes, and a smile that was so big it made her eyes squint. She was the mother of three daughters and spoke of them with such pride. Her office was decorated in colorings by her daughters, and photos of her family and friends. Files covered her desk so much that you could barely make out the color of it. The office naturally was dull, but you could tell she tried to add color to it as best she could. This told me something about her personality—she always tried to see the positive, the color in dark situations. Her dream was to help others, and that in itself says enough about who Ally is.

As I began to organize her office, we got to chatting. An hour into the conversation, we were laughing, talking about my ridiculous dating experiences, and everything in between. I told her how I recently got a dating app and told her my tag line I used to lure men in: "You have great bone structure." We both laughed, and she told me more about her life and her work in advocacy. Then she pulled a brilliant move, starting with a series of questions.

Ally: "What are you getting your degree in?"

Me: "Media Communications."

Ally: "Do you like it?"

Me: "I love it. I dropped out of school a few years ago, but I love learning now that I'm older."

She continued asking me straight questions, back to back.

Ally: "What College do you go to again?"

Me: "NC State"

Ally: "How long have you been a nanny?"

Me: "Around five years for the same family."

Ally: "And when were you diagnosed?"

Me: "Around 20."

It took me about 30 seconds to realize what I just said. I put my hand on my head and started laughing. "Nice move," I said with a smile. "I'll have to remember that on my next date when I want to dig deeper." She smiled and pulled up a chair, "Tell me more."

Ally and I fell into a deep conversation, and that is when I opened up about my story and diagnosis. It was the first time I had spoken about it to anyone outside of my immediate family. Seeing her relentless dedication to making a difference in the mental health community inspired me. Soon she convinced me to speak at a local mental health conference about my experience. I couldn't believe that I agreed, but I did.

On the day of the conference, I woke up and got ready to go. I will never forget my outfit. A mint green high waisted skirt with a beautiful cropped flowered blouse, and nude heels. I was calm, a little too calm, but on the drive over, I could feel my palms sweating and my stomach-turning.

There were a lot of people at the conference—advocates, psychologists, therapists, students, and people from all over. I paced nervously around watching the clock tick by. Amid a daze, I felt a woman tap on my shoulder, "Are you, Hannah?" I shook my head, yes. "You will be speaking in about 30 minutes." She quickly walked away to her next task.

I stood still for a moment and then started walking towards the room, but about one minute into my walk, I turned around and ran into the bathroom. I vomited up for about five minutes straight and sat on the cold floor of the bathroom in my pretty mint green skirt. I felt awful. I felt ashamed. Why was I here? I thought. What was I doing? I thought I was so close to being normal why the fuck would I decide to do this? My boyfriend at the time was against it, and it didn't seem logical that I would open up to a crowd of strangers. So what was I doing sitting on the bathroom floor, with vomit on my flowered shirt, five minutes away from talking about the most shameful part of my life? It was the most uncomfortable I had ever been. I finally stood up, washed up, and walked out of the bathroom.

I debated leaving, but then I saw Ally with a huge smile waving to me. I couldn't let her down. She believed in me and worked so hard to get me a spot because she had a "gut feeling" as she put it, about me. So I did the talk. I'll give you a brief summary of how it went.

In the ten minutes on stage, I spoke, I cried, I laughed, I cried some more, I stopped, paused, and it finally ended. During the talk, I even admitted to the audience that it was my first time opening up. I was so emotional that a woman with PTSD even came up to comfort me. It was a wreck. It was brutal. I was mortified. After it ended, I quickly walked out of the room and through the doors. I sat in a hallway for about twenty minutes crying, but I got up, grabbed my purse, and started to exit the building.

Then I heard someone call my name, it was one of the women running the conference. With excitement in her voice, she said, "Come here quickly!" It pained me to stay any longer. But I walked towards the woman and into a large room filled with booths of different organizations and businesses. The room was loud, and there were lots of people. One booth, in particular, had a long line of people waiting. She walked me over to a spot where I just stood. At that point, I was just moving without thinking. I was looking towards the ground, and my mind was so cluttered with negative thoughts. I felt so uncomfortable.

"Hannah, this is Ashley," the woman said. I looked up. A teenage girl with long curly brown hair stood in front of me, and then there was a man behind her, and then another man behind him, and then another girl behind him and so on.

I looked to the woman who brought me in, "Wait, are these people…. are these people here for me?" She softly smiled at me like I was a child. "Yes, Hannah, these people are here to speak with you." The line I initially saw was not for a booth; it was for me.

One by one, people came up to me. Some cried, others asked questions, and some people just came to say, "Thank you!" At first, I was uncomfortable, but when I spoke to each person, it came very naturally. I was open, and so were they. Every experience was different, and I listened carefully to every word uttered. A father who had lost his daughter to suicide, a young college student struggling with depression, an older woman diagnosed with bipolar whose husband had just left her, and so on. Every person was beautiful, every story made an impact. These people thought I was brave, but they were the brave ones. I was so inspired and in awe of the people there, people with a mental illness.

We were there together. It was one of the most beautiful experiences of my life, and it taught me the power of truth. These were my people; this was my path, and my life changed that day.

*Truth is discomfort.*

It's uncomfortable to realize that you need to go to therapy. It's uncomfortable, to be honest with your partner about your feelings. It's uncomfortable to open up to your family and friends about what you are going through. Being open and honest is not comfortable.

It's uncomfortable when people ask me details about my life. It's uncomfortable when I am hanging out with friends, and multiple people give me their theories on why mental illness doesn't exist. It's uncomfortable talking about self-harming, knowing that my mother and father are listening. It's uncomfortable when people ask why I haven't slept or why I am distant. It's uncomfortable when a mother reaches out to me about her 12-year-old son who committed suicide right in front of her. It's uncomfortable telling people that I am not okay. It's uncomfortable.

We have this idea that everything we do in life has to be comfortable to be right, but that's not true. I used to feel so uncomfortable opening up about bipolar disorder that I would throw up before speaking engagements. In fact, I still do sometimes, but I always get on stage and speak. The more I have walked in my truth, the more confidence I built in my broken. The main reason is that I see so many people suffering both with and without a mental illness. Now I thrive in discomfort. It's where I feel the most comfortable now because discomfort is where my truth lies.

We all experience discomfort. The question is—Would you rather be uncomfortable pretending to be someone you are not, or would you rather be uncomfortable being who you are, being open and honest?

Truth is discomfort, but guess what else is uncomfortable—loving ourselves. Loving and embracing what makes you different is not comfortable, especially in the beginning, but what overshadows that feeling is the freedom you feel. If being open and honest was comfortable, everyone would be doing it.

Truth is discomfort, and it's time we get uncomfortable and start loving the unfixed version of ourselves.

# PART: Finding Our Purpose

*It wasn't until the seed of the tree realized that it was capable of providing shade, shelter, and natural beauty to the world that it was finally able to blossom. Its purpose lead to its growth.*

One time a 16-year-old boy came up to me after I spoke at a conference about my experience living with bipolar disorder. He told me that he was struggling to accept his diagnosis of bipolar and dealing with depression. His parents sent him to a wellness treatment center over the summer, they changed his diet, got him a personal trainer, and a therapist. However, none of it was working. He asked me with tears in his eyes,

"Am I supposed to hate myself?"

I told him that he did not have to feel the need to hate everything about himself just because he was different.

I didn't ask him to tell me more about his diagnosis because I am not a doctor, and I didn't believe that would help him. Instead,

I asked him about his life outside of mental illness. He immediately perked up, revealing his passion for video games and comic books. It quickly came to me, and I asked him to pull up a chair.

We discussed his passion more in-depth and how he could mold that into a way for him to visually see his emotions and give him hope. We searched for different online video tutorials for him to learn more about graphic design. I told him to make a comic book, and create a story based on the battle he was facing—a story about perseverance and turning his emotions into both the villain and the hero.

A year later I received an email from him with an attachment. He had created a comic book and shared it with other people who struggled with depression in the video gaming community. He went on to tell me that he felt empowered, and it motivated him to go to a doctor. It was one of the best emails I have ever received.

The fact is his emotions would always be present. My advice was not based around trying to rid himself of the pain, but learning to build it into something much more significant. I wanted him to do something that would empower him enough to believe that he could live a good life. I wanted to give him something that would help him gain the confidence to seek out the treatment he needed without feeling so ashamed. I wanted him to love himself.

There is a purpose to our problems.

Self-love comes with self-service, and if you can take your pain and turn it into something to help others, including yourself, you begin to see the beauty in who you are in the present. If it were not for my emotions, if it were not for the battles I face both presently and in the past, I would not be able to create the way that I do.

The unfixed version of self-love is about gaining confidence in what makes you different. It doesn't cure us of insecurities, no, but it gives our pain a purpose.

Create a vision board, write down what you are passionate about, utilize the resources available to you. If you love to cook, take a cooking class, or self-publish a cookbook based on your emotions. Self-publishing has never been easier, so use it to your benefit. Create a workbook for people struggling with self-love. Make a Pinterest account where you can share your ideas. You don't have to turn it into a career.

We have to spend more energy on building ourselves up instead of breaking ourselves down. It reduces the shame we feel and inspires us to be more open.

Grab your journal. Remember, when you are writing, forget about structure, format or spelling. This is a sacred place for your truth to be exposed. Just let your mind and emotions speak to your pen. Here are some prompts for you to reflect on, and they go in order:

Why do you struggle to love yourself? What lesson or message can you take from the pain of not loving yourself? What would you say to a young girl or boy who was in the position you are in? What can you teach others? Write it out after reading this part of the book.

Know this…

Your scars tell a story.

When we give love to others, we give love to ourselves.

We see the beauty in the small things, the beauty of each other.

# PART: Stop Saying I'm Sorry

*I forgave myself a long time ago for my imperfections. Now I value them over other people's opinions.*

*I'm sorry.* Two words that I have said *too* much, and you probably have as well. It's okay. Apologizing for who I am and what I feel used to be a daily habit alongside brushing my teeth. I have seen people treat others horribly, but seem to fit in better than I do. Their behavior is accepted. If you are cruel to others and judge harshly, then those are qualities that will wither you. If you are kind, and you give to others you shouldn't feel ashamed for being a version of human that people are unwilling to accept.

Why is it we have to be so willing to accept the imperfections, mistakes, and differences of others, but we don't receive the same in return?

People love us until they have to make an effort; that's all it is. It takes effort to understand what you do not understand. People will

63

use whatever label they can as a platform to blame us and get out of the situation appearing as the hero, and we sit there wallowing in our emotions as the villain once again.

I used to let people voice their negative beliefs about people with mental illness freely, and I thought it made me open-minded, but it didn't. I was scared to speak the truth because that message goes against what a lot of people are preaching. The more I grew online and on social media, the more suffering I saw. The support I receive from those living with a mental illness is consumed in pure love. People who are literally at rock bottom taking time every single day to post a comment or send a message to empower me. These are the empaths, the misunderstood. They give me the words that people have stolen from them, and that's not insane, that's absolutely beautiful. However, they wake up in the pain of shame. They have to apologize for simply being, and that's fucking bullshit.

People treat animals with more respect than they do people with a mental illness. Animals protect their community; humans could care less about theirs. So I stopped playing nice because I didn't take this leap to play by the rules, the rules that suppress people who are struggling. I came to make and live by my own, and so did you.

Stand up for what you believe and, most importantly, stand up for who you are. Stand up for your right to live a good life, one where you feel comfortable to seek the treatment or resources you need.

Imagine yourself as a child. Stand up for that girl or boy that is being bullied. The child who is being suffocated by their emotions but can't be honest because they're scared. They feel ashamed of who they are.

When you see yourself as a kid, you don't see evil or bad, do you? You see the purity and maybe a child who is just lost in the woods begging for someone to help them. Stand up for them, because you are strong enough and bright enough to do so.

The unfixed version of self-love is when we stop putting our self-worth in undeserving hands and asking for forgiveness from undeserving mouths. Today is the day we let go of what's holding us back from loving ourselves. Today is the day we stop apologizing for being different; for being human.

# PART: You Are a Real Queen

*A real Queen is courageous. A real Queen empowers others to love themselves even as she struggles to do the same. A real Queen is a survivor. You are a real Queen. You wear an invisible crown every day, not just for a moment, but for eternity.*

**This is Susanna's Story, I call it: *A Real Queen***

It's the most cherished story and the most important voice I keep with me; and that's the voice of a young girl I met in the mental hospital. Her name is Susanna. It is the story that taught me the importance of redefining the word "broken."

"Hannah, this is Susanna. She is going to be rooming with you." I looked over to see a young girl with frazzled hair and eyes swollen. She could barely stand. She kept her head down as I approached her.

I was taken aback by how young Susanna was, and I could tell she was absolutely petrified, so I approached her gently instead of as my normal over-the-top-energetic self.

"Hey Susanna! I'm Hannah, and your new best friend." Her head rose slowly with a slight smile, and finally, she looked at me. From that point on, Susanna accompanied me everywhere, not that there were many places to go. I've never had a little sister, but that's what Susanna was to me, even though we only crossed paths for a moment in time.

Susanna lived with schizophrenia. She had been in and out of mental hospitals for the majority of her youth. She didn't commit any crime, but coming from an extremely religious family, Susanna was an outcast, and forced to live with her grandmother who struggled to take care of her. The only life she was familiar with was one that was kept behind white walls, away from society.

She was a talented artist. With only crayons, Susanna could turn a blank sheet of paper into a masterpiece. She also loved poetry, and during the time we had to ourselves, she would share her writings, which were profoundly deep. Susanna admired me, though at the time I felt undeserving of such admiration.

She wanted to know everything about my life. There was one topic in particular she wanted to discuss—boys. Susanna would be giddy with joy when I would tell her stories about crushes, high school, and romance. At night she asked me questions until she fell asleep.

"Hannah," I heard her whisper one night from her bed.

Susanna: "Have you ever had, you know, S E X."

Me: "Sex? Have I ever had sex before? Yes. I've definitely had S E X before!"

Every question was followed up with, "What's it like?"

She was fascinated that I was nominated for Prom Queen in high school. Susanna had never been to a school dance or any of the events that most of us take for granted—the dress, the hair, the music, and everything that takes place at Proms.

One night Susanna decided to share more of her story with me. She lifted her shirt, and my heart dropped. As much as I wanted to cry, I didn't want Susanna to feel uncomfortable. The words, "Help me," were carved up and down her arm. She was only 13 years old.

One day Susanna was upset because a close family member was a no-show at visitation, which made her feel ashamed and abandoned. As I sat in the community room, drawing on paper with the other patients, an idea popped into my head.

I walked around the room and sat next to her, "Let's draw the dress you would wear to Prom." She lit up with excitement.

Over the next couple of days, Susanna would draw everything that she wanted for her future. Several sheets of paper were decorated with everything from dresses to her dream boy. She hugged me every time I praised or complimented her.

One afternoon while we were playing cards, I told Susanna she was beautiful, to which she replied, "I've never been told that before." My heart broke. All girls deserve to be told they are beautiful. I think Susanna was living outside of those white walls for once.

I finally received my release date from the hospital. Susanna was happy but sad at the same time. It was frowned upon that patients make any effort to keep in touch with other patients in the facility. I reminded her daily that even though I was leaving, we would always be close, and that hopefully one day we would cross paths again.

It was what happened on my last day there that forever changed my life.

During recreation time in the backyard of the hospital Susanna, some of the women, and I sat chatting on the old picnic bench. It was a beautiful day with no humidity, which was rare during summer in the South. Susanna sat on the ground quietly as I braided her hair. In the midst of my conversation with one of the girls, I felt Susanna abruptly grab my hand.

I looked to her, "Is everything alright Susanna?"

The tone of her voice told me that it was serious, and something had been on her mind.

"Can I ask you something?" She paused, "But you must promise to tell me the truth."

I gently touched her shoulder, "Of course, Susanna."

She looked down towards the ground and then back to me again, "I'm not going to Prom, am I, Hannah?"

I felt my stomach drop to the ground.

All the girls went silent, including me. It felt like time had stopped as we endured the heartbreak of Susanna's question. We knew the answer was No. The reality of Susanna's circumstances would not allow her to go to a public school where things like Prom took place. I was not going to lie to Susanna. I was going to tell her the truth.

"No Susanna. You aren't going to go to Prom."

I choked up but pulled myself together. I knew the pain of hearing my answer was present in her, but that was not the truth I wanted her to take with her. It was this one:

"Prom and high school, all those things you think make you special; they don't. There is so much more you are going to do in life that is far better than Prom. You don't have to go to Prom to justify your beauty, to believe that you are special. You are better than a Prom Queen, you are Susanna."

Susanna smiled, and I continued to braid her hair.

The day came for me to say goodbye. Susanna and I hugged each other with tears in our eyes. She made me promise that I would keep her story and share it someday. It was almost as if she knew where my path was taking me.

Susanna was so bright. She was an artist, but she wore a label of "broken," and society punished her for it. Society punished us all there for it. Susanna needed treatment, but she didn't need to be fixed. I realized the importance of self-love and what it means to embrace what makes you different. It gives you the power to believe in yourself, to remind yourself of your beauty when the world does not. She could see people in a way that others could not, and I saw her.

Before I left, I placed a note on Susanna's pillow with a crown I had made from tissue. If you follow my quotes in social media, this one may be familiar.

*A real Queen is courageous. A real Queen empowers others to love themselves even when she struggles to do the same. A real Queen is a survivor. You are a Queen. You wear an invisible crown every day, not just for a moment, but for eternity.*

We toss the word "self-love" around without explaining what it really means. Self-love isn't about getting to a place where you love yourself, it's about loving yourself in the place *you are in.*

Being that I live with a mental illness, I have seen firsthand the damage that phrases like "Fixing yourself" or "You can be someone better" have on people.

When Susanna wore that crown made out of toilet paper, I asked her how she felt, "I really love myself right now." She whispered it to me as a secret—as if she told me she murdered someone, because loving herself was *wrong*. And the reason it pained me was that it was short-lived, because the moment she walked out of that hospital, she was going to be told the opposite.

Susanna has impacted my life on so many different levels—when I looked back in my journal years after being released, I saw the page entitled "Susanna," and I remembered that promise I made to her, and to myself, of sharing her story and that of others. No human should go through life believing that just because they are different, they are undeserving of self-love. This is untrue—and the world needs to know this truth.

# PART: Meet Me Halfway

*It was when I ran away from the girl everyone expected me to be that I ran into the woman I was meant to be. And I heard her say, "There you are, I was nervous you wouldn't show."*

In January 2016, I published the content I decided to open up about my bipolar disorder and created my blog, *Halfway2Hannah*. I have been asked many times why I chose this name, but I've kept quiet because, like everything, there is a story behind it, one I want to share on my own in this book.

I was months away from graduating from college, getting my degree in an area that I was passionate about, Media Communication. I had a couple of great offers to build a career in Marketing and Communication on a corporate level.

Although life was great, and my path seemed clear, I felt an emptiness inside of me. I knew that if I accepted one of the job offers, the blog I had been manifesting in my Google docs over the last two years would stay hidden. I wouldn't be able to fully reveal my diagnosis of bipolar, and everything would be left behind me. I was being pulled in two directions—one that made sense, and one that did not make sense. I battled with it for months. Life was normal, so why was I questioning it? Wasn't moving on and going on the straight path what I wanted?

It wasn't a small decision; it was one of the most significant decisions I've ever had to make. Financially speaking, there was no money in it for me. Advocates get paid nothing, which is another huge problem. My chances of getting a job would be cut in half. It was a considerable risk, but there was something inside of me that kept saying "Do it, and don't look back."

One night I started reading all the content I had been building up. When I came across something I wrote about in my journals I immediately knew what I had to do at that moment. I was going to find *the journal*—the one I kept prior to, during, and right after the mental hospital.

Several months after being released from the hospital, I felt the urge to throw out the journal. Fortunately, I decided to hide it away in my childhood bureau that was located in the back of the storage room kept for my family's items. I drove out to my mother's home in the middle of the night and went into the mess of the storage room. It took a long time, but finally I made my way to my bureau. In it were various items from my childhood, which I entertained myself with before opening the bottom drawer. When I did—there it was, an old hot-pink spiral notebook with stickers on the front and back. It had been six years since I opened the journal, but I knew there was something in it I needed to see. When I opened it, my writings, both dark and humorous, deep and light, covered the pages. Stories, experiences, people, drawings, thoughts, poems, and quotes filled every page. I sat there for hours reading over every word.

I saw how sick I was, and the extent of where my emotional turmoil took me. But those pages were not filled with pain, they were filled with the most powerful thing I have in this world—my truth. These were the most important chapters of my life. I closed my eyes, laid back on the concrete floor and allowed my mind to create a visual that would help me make my decision to either come forward or move on.

*The vision...*

I was walking down a road, and at the halfway point I arrived— between doing what made me fixed, what made me right, what made me "normal," and what left me *broken*—the past, the emotions, the people, the shame, the messiness, and the diagnosis of bipolar. Looking ahead on the paved road, I saw hands waving me forward—but before taking that next step, I stopped and did something I was not supposed to do—I turned around to see the turmoil that existed behind me. But when I turned, I saw something much more beautiful.

The shattered pieces that made up the road behind me were beautifully put together. I saw the chapters of my life that are the foundation of my story. I saw the people who sacrificed their scars in hopes to heal mine. I saw purpose. When I broke, my truth was exposed because it's in my broken that I found...me. If I had continued forward, I would not be writing this book because part of that road ahead prohibited my ability to create. I would utilize my expertise with the intent of making money and doing what was considered to be right.

It was at the *halfway* point that for the first time I trusted myself, I believed in myself and my story, so I stopped moving forward, grabbed a shovel and dug my own road. A road where I did utilize my talents to do the right thing while wearing the label of wrong proudly. It was at the *halfway* point that I was no longer a stranger to myself. I saw the girl I was meant to be, and she whispered to me gently,

"There you are, I was nervous you wouldn't show."

*Halfway2Hannah.*

# PART: The Story of the Storm

*My story is not a sad story, it's a real one. It's a story about a girl who fought through a storm she thought would never end.*

I woke up in a cloud. My vision was blurry, and my head heavy and throbbing. I didn't remember falling asleep. I blinked my eyes several times, unable to make out the people standing around me. It appeared as if everyone was underwater. Was I dreaming? I lifted my head up slowly when I heard my father's voice in the distance. Things slowly began to become a little clearer, and I could make out some of what my father was saying. I heard him say, "You mean to tell me…" When my father started a sentence with these five words it meant my brothers and I were in deep shit, which is why I perked up with fear. In an instant everything became unclouded. It was like someone flipped on the light and turned up the music. A fucked-up version of a surprise party.

Everything went from slow motion to high speed, as if someone hit the "play" button on life again. I felt more coherent but not enough to speak up. I observed my surroundings. In front of my bed stood a doctor staring down at his chart, talking to a nurse. To my far right was the nurse who'd been with me the previous night, coming in often to chat and fill my IV with something that would "ease my anxiety." I looked to my left, and there stood a police officer. She looked angry—the type of person that could be celebrating the most joyous occasion but still wears a face of dissatisfaction.

It was hard for me to move. As I found out later, it was due to the heavy sedatives that were meant to "ease my anxiety." I felt betrayed by the nurse, who had opened up about her dating life, or lack thereof, throughout the night. By 1 AM I learned that Jimmy, who she met on Plentyoffish.com never called her back after they went to the $1.99 pizza buffet. She thought he was into her, but his text shortly after that night was just emojis. And Sally, her best friend, had been on a date with him as well, and there was tension in their friendship. Useless chatter all night. My dad's presence was my anchor.

To the far left, I saw another police officer standing with a doctor and my father. The three of them in a circle, but extremely close to one another. My father's body language and his stance emphasized my concern that something wasn't right—his hand placed on his chin, as if he was pondering something in anger, arms crossed tightly, his legs apart and his jaw clenched—the look on his face can be summed up in one word—*fear*—a word that I had never used in describing my dad. I felt paralyzed with fear and guilt but slowly started to piece together what must have happened.

I had walked into the Emergency Room the night before with

my mother, asking to speak with a doctor because I didn't feel well mentally. My mother and I were placed in a separate waiting room in the back with a few other people. *Remember I met Missy and her father in the waiting room.* It was flu season, so the beds throughout the emergency room were packed. At one point I got a bed, my mother left when my dad came to the hospital to sit with me. I must have gotten up during the night, completely unaware of what I was doing, and hurt someone on staff. I couldn't remember the specifics. I had no idea that I had become so ill that I would act out violently towards someone else. It was evident that I had no control over what I was doing anymore. I had indeed gone insane.

I looked back at the female officer sitting close to me and quietly whispered to her, "Ma'am," which in the South is a polite way to grab a woman's attention. She looked up at me, and then looked down. It was as if I were invisible. A nurse came in, to check my vitals, and I again asked, "What's going on? Please, tell me something." He looked down at me, took off the tight blood pressure arm wrap, glanced at the officer and back to me, saying nothing. I looked toward my father, silently screaming with my eyes for help. His hands were moving everywhere as he spoke to the doctor and the other officer. I heard the word "lawyer" mentioned, which made it even more evident that I had done something illegal. As I began to weep, I felt the female officer's ice-cold hands touch my arm to help me out of bed.

I was dressed in a hospital gown. Then I heard a jingle, and noticed she was taking out handcuffs. At the time I didn't know who I'd hurt, and the guilt was suffocating. Finally, my father walked away from the conversation, and the other officer came up to me. I felt like I was in and out of consciousness while he spoke, the feeling of shock began to take over. The only thing I could make out was something close to "...you have been taken under the custody of the State...you are going to an undisclosed location...no further contact with your parents." I was finally close to my father which gave me comfort, but the man who had seemed impossible to break was slowly cracking, and the pain I felt from that moment has never left me.

I broke down in tears with my arms behind my back, talking out loud to my father, who was walking next to me as I stepped outside towards the cop car with the female officer. I had no idea what I'd done. I had no idea where I was going. I started screaming out repeatedly, "I'm so sorry, Dad!" I repeated it over and over again, my eyes shut tightly, hoping that if I apologized enough maybe God would give me a second chance. My Dad ran up quickly and calmed me for a moment. I opened my eyes, and the officer made it clear that we only had a minute to talk before I would be taken away.

"Dad tell me what I did, I have to know. I knew something was wrong with..."

He stopped me, and I opened my eyes, staring into the face of the toughest man I know, who was falling apart. He persevered through everything and always got the job done, but this time was different. It was all out of his control. His eyes began filling up with tears, again a sight I had never seen before, but he composed himself, cleared his throat.

"No, no, Hannah, you didn't do anything. You didn't hurt anyone last night. Nothing. You fell asleep two hours after I got there, and the police came in around 6 AM, but you didn't do anything to anybody. I'm not sure what's going on..."

His voice started cracking, "...but your mother and I are going to figure it out. I love you. It's going to be alright." I was confused. The officer began tugging at my arm, and I looked at her with anger, "Wait! Where the hell am I going? I don't get it."

She said with a stern voice, "The officer explained to you before, we are going to the undisclosed location..."

She put me in the back of the cop car and shut the door. The windows were closed, but I looked out at my Dad. He waved good-bye to me with a semi-smile to ease my anxiety. The cuffs had been taken off my hands, and as the car began to move forward, I touched the window, mouthing back before he was out of my sight, "I love you. I'm sorry."

I put my head on the glass window, closing my eyes and pray-ing silently to someone, some higher existence outside of me, and asked for help; let this be my last sleep. I watched the trees quickly go by outside my window. When we passed a field of daises, my mind drifted to a time when I was a child.

When I was around five, my grandparents took me on a road trip with them along the east coast. It was spring. At one-point Nana and Grampy pulled over with their camper by a field filled with daises. I remember walking through the field and the bright yellow color made me feel like I was in a dream at the time. My grandmother took a photo of me that still goes everywhere with her. That child was happy, so in love with life—but obviously, that girl no longer existed. She had been crippled by her own emotions and the pressure of society to be something more than who she already was. I closed my eyes and finally allowed my broken to consume me. I would be taken to a mental hospital and released twenty days later with a diagnosis of bipolar disorder.

This was the moment that I believed was the end, but little did I know, it was only the beginning. The broken pieces created an opening to the next part of my journey.

# PART: The Truth About Broken

*What we believe to be the end is usually just the beginning.*

The part of my story that I believed was a dead end, in reality, was a beautiful start to my becoming the person I was always meant to be, and to love that person. It put me on a path towards manifesting my purpose and creating life purely based around my truth. If you are struggling with self-love, struggling to find happiness, don't worry, you are not alone. There is no shame in being human, and the human you are right now in this moment, whether you are at the peak of your career or barely making enough money to pay rent, you are still deserving of self-love. If you are in the best shape of your life or are still fighting bad habits, you are still deserving of self-love.

We have to stop waiting on self-love to happen when we are at a certain point in our life—when people accept us for who we are or what we have. You are allowed to love yourself as you are.

Broken is not wrong, bad or damaged—broken is an opening for our truth. It is an opening that cannot be fixed or covered up and it shouldn't be.

The experiences that I thought were supposed to set me back were actually launching me forward. It is the people who are seen as *broken* who have given me the gift of *purpose*. The reality of where life has taken me thus far is ten times better than the life I planned for. I wouldn't change one thing.

Broken is what makes us real. I will always be a little messy, all over the place and ridiculous. Sometimes I am low, other times I am high. I love myself even when I hate myself. Maybe that doesn't make sense right now, but it will.

I could wither in my problems, I could become a victim of what has happened to me in the past, but I choose not to because I see the light in those dark moments of my life. I could hide in the shadows of others' distorted perception of who I truly am, but I choose not to. I want you to come out of the shadows and live the life you deserve.

Stories are not meant to be glamorous; they are intended to be real. You have a story, and it started the day were born. Your story matters because you matter and what you feel matters as well.

Creating a story is about doing your best to live every day, even if all you could do was open your eyes. There will and have been parts of my story that will be more difficult than others, but where one chapter ends, another begins.

Your broken pieces are there in front of you. You've been looking at them with disdain, shame, disgust, and anger. It's time for that to change. Give yourself the chance to love who you are as you are.

I hope I have inspired you to love and embrace what makes you different—the unfixed version of you is the best version of you. I hope you can redefine broken; not as bad or damaged goods, but as truth and beauty.

You are a mosaic of human; a masterpiece that doesn't exist without being shattered along the way.

This is your *truth*. This is your *broken*.

Now create the masterpiece of *you*.

# The Words You Inspire

You are my forever muses of inspiration. I wouldn't be here without you. I am not on the podium lecturing you; I am sitting next to you as your friend, sister, and peer. We are in this together.

The following pages feature my quotes, poems, and writings.

Emotions don't make you weak, they make you fearless. Because those who feel more, fear less.

It's okay to be different. It's okay to feel broken.
It's okay to feel too much in a world that feels too little.

On her dark days, she screamed.
On her bright days, she laughed.
There was no in between,
but every day she felt.

Sometimes instead of saying, "Just keep a positive mindset!" What we need to hear is, "I know this f*cking sucks right now, but you're a badass, and you're going to push through it. This moment will make you better.

## This One's for the Life of the Party

There are many different faces and personalities of mental illness. This one is for the life of the party.

The people who stand out in a crowd, these are the ones that go unnoticed because their ability to be so gravitating and boldly exist overshadows the fact that they are misunderstood and alone in a world that thinks they're fine.

The problem is, one day, you can no longer simply remain in character. One day the part of you that makes you stand out in a crowd will also be the part of you that has the power to break you down.

I used to stand out in a way that made me believe I was truly living, but in reality, I was standing out in a way that kept others from seeing my truth. I was standing out, but I wasn't looking in.

Because here's what I know, the longer you ignore that there is a problem, the more damage you are doing to yourself. The highs and lows will get worse, and they will become more present, and one by one, people leave the crowd that at one time you stood out in, and then you're alone.

Be vibrant and unique in a way that makes you feel alive. Share your truth and find the people who will love you for it. The people who are there for you whether you are dancing or shattering, smiling or crumbling,

Because the things that make you different, the parts that people say make you unlovable or flawed are the most powerful parts of you. Confidence is rooted in what makes us different, the parts of us that others label as flaws. You are more than the life of the party. You are real, and that's the most beautiful thing about you.

This is my truth. I fall too hard, I love too much, and I feel everything that comes my way. I live with bipolar, so I get what it's like to feel misunderstood, but I can finally say that I am no longer pretending to be someone I am not.

I am more than the life of the party.

And so are you.

When people ask, "How do you feel?" I usually reply with the truth,

"Everything."

We all mess up. We all make mistakes.
We all could have gone about a situation better.
It doesn't make us bad. It makes us human.

Openness is a gift.

It invites others to find beauty in what makes them different, what makes them broken, and there is nothing more magical than giving the gift of unapologetic self-love.

You can practice wellness, read self-help books, and meditate on mountain tops, those are all beautiful practices and experiences—but if you are looking for these methods to erase your insecurities, to wash away your pain, to cure your mental illness, you are setting yourself up for disappointment. Broken is where your truth is exposed. So stop beating yourself down for being different, for feeling conflicted, or insecure.

You are not bad; you are human.

May you always live louder than others, feel emotions so deeply, and love yourself for everything you once believed made you flawed.

Sometimes the light we are desperately searching for is found by being present in the dark and finding the light that exists within us.

I don't know who lied to you, but I'm not in recovery, because
I don't have a broken arm,
I have a mental illness. I don't want you to fix me, because I
don't need to be fixed.
I need to be accepted.

My mental illness is never going away, so stop telling me to change
my mindset. Stop telling me that the downward dog will save me.
Stop making me feel the need to f*cking apologize for being
different. I've accepted my broken; I love it. I would never change
the way that I was born.

Your problem with me is no longer my problem with me.

Our biggest rival in life is the person in our reflection.

When someone says, "I'm fine!" It usually means,

"I'm a mess. But I have no fucking clue how to respond without feeling embarrassed and ashamed."

## When You Feel Too Much

For so long, I felt suffocated by the surface of life and wanted to desperately escape. I felt like in order for people to love me, I had to fix myself.

At one point, I realized I could no longer suppress my emotions, but I could stop punishing myself for feeling them in the first place. I decided to love those parts of myself labeled as wrong, and that's when I saw the beauty of feeling, the magic of loving too much, or loving too hard.

You are allowed to love what makes you different. If people don't accept you, let them go and tell them,

*If you want to see the stars, you must be willing to travel through the dark.*

People with a mental illness think they must hide who they are
if they want to be accepted,
so the question is,

Who is truly insane?

The person who hides or
The person who makes them feel the need to hide?

Believe in the beauty of becoming.
Believe in the power of growth.
But most importantly believe in yourself.

Even on those rainy days where it feels like the world is covered in grey, do not lose hope, because there has never been a storm that lasted forever. The sun is always present; it too has to find its way through the clouds.

## Mother Nature

Our emotions have the power to distort our reflection.

They can blind us to the beauty of who we are and what we are capable of providing to the world. What we feel often becomes what we believe, but it doesn't have to. If I could tell you anything it would be to love yourself whole even when you feel less than half.

Speak to yourself differently—with kindness instead of shame or hate. We cannot always control our emotions, or what our mind is telling us, but we can control the way we speak to them.

We can control how we perceive our emotions as an essential part of who we are. A part that doesn't make us bad, but that makes us human.

I look at my emotions, similar to the way I perceive mother nature. An unpredictable part of the Universe that is both beautiful and destructive at the same time.

Because like a tree, we grow from the ground up. Leaves will fall, and branches will break, but even in those moments, it still provides beauty to this world. So do not give up on all that you are and all that you could be for where you are or what you feel in this moment.

Our strength and power still exist even when we cannot see it.

Outward appearances can be deceiving.

Appearances can trick us into believing that someone has it all, but many who appear full of life are tragically empty of it inside.

Your body is a work of art. Always remember that my dear—
you are an artist, and your body is a masterpiece.

You cannot enjoy the beauty of a rose if you do not admire its thorns. You cannot look in awe of a rainbow without respecting the storm that set it free. Take me for both my beauty and my thorns or leave me as I am.

I hate that there are so many people out there who are struggling and feel trapped by their own emotions. You feel so alone. But to those people who feel that way right now, I am here to tell you that you f*cking matter in this world. You are not irrelevant.

Your story is important. It is beautiful just like you.

I will meet you in the aftermath of the storm dancing in the puddles of our pain.

They told me to pursue acting, and I replied,

"I live with a mental illness. I've been an actress my whole life."

You are not flawed.

You care in a world that prides itself on not giving a fuck.

Take pride in your ability to love unconditionally.

I am not ashamed of my mental illness. I am ashamed of those who contribute to the stigma that steals so many beautiful souls away from us every single day.

Ignorance is shameful, not the way I was made.

It was when I was lost that suddenly I felt found.

Beautiful soul—My hope for you is that one day, you can finally be at peace with your reflection; you can finally see that your beauty exists in what you believe makes you flawed.

Breaking and rebuilding happen simultaneously. So when you are crumbling and think the world is crashing down, remember it's from the bottom that we rise again.

I'm not going to change myself to fit into this world. I'm going to change the world that makes me feel the pressure to fit in.

# Photography & Design

Book Cover Design by Donna Adi (@donna_adi)
Thank you Donna. You have such a special gift and you made my dream come true with this cover.

Book Cover Photo by Jillian Clark (@itsjillianclark)
Thank you Jillian. You are a beautiful soul and one of the most talented photographers. I am so grateful.

About the Author Photo by Ofer Yakov (@ofer_yakov)
Thank you Ofer. You captured my Wonderland in this photo, and I am forever grateful.

# Acknowledgements

Writing has been a dream of mine since I was a child. Along this journey, I have met people near and far who have inspired me and my writing. If it were not for these people, I would not be who or where I am today.

My beautiful Nana, Fran Onishuk, and Grampy, Daniel Onishuk. There are no words to truly describe what your love has meant to me. You are my heart always.

My brothers who are the reason I am who I am today. Erik Blum, you are one of the most special human beings and I am blessed to call you my brother. Jordan Blum, the way you perceive the world inspires me, I love you. My beautiful sisters-in-law Carmen Blum and Lauren DeMasi. Melissa Blum and Rachel Blum, my cousins but more like my sisters, thank you for loving me as I am.

My fireflies, the souls who give me light when I am in the dark. Emmett, Minna, Nolan, Ayla, Hannah Grace, Daniel, Madison, Ava.

My Aunt, Andrea Randall, you have loved me for exactly who I am since the day I was born. You have supported me throughout this journey. You are my aunt, my sister, and my best friend. Thank you. My Uncle David and my cousins Alec and Garrett, and their dog Benny (my aunt wanted me to say that).

My beautiful friends who are truly my soulmates and have supported me throughout this journey. Nadine Weiss, Anya Knower, Courtney Jones, Jenny Davis, Sophie Dugan, Caroline Craven, Nora Poulsen, Ivy Warren, Bianca Parker and all my friends who have supported me. Sarah Snow, I wouldn't be here without you. You are a gift to the world, and my life.

The Onishuk and Blum family. My aunts and uncles—Rob and Diana, Mark, Danny and Lynne. My aunt Jessica Schwartz.

In memory of my late Aunty Bev.

My beautiful and kindhearted cousin Alexa Onishuk. My loving cousins Yuri, Nicole, Linsey, & Nick.

All the mental health advocates out there working every day to change the world. You inspire me. A special thanks to one advocate in particular who is my friend as well, Donita Cline. Thank you for supporting me from day 1.

In memory of a friend who will forever have a place in my heart, #34.

# Sources

"The Starry Night, 1889 by Vincent Van Gogh." *10 Facts That You Don›t Know About «Starry Night» by Vincent Van Gogh,* https://www.vincentvangogh.org/starry-night.jsp.

# About The Author

HANNAH BLUM is a writer, content creator and mental health advocate. In 2016 Hannah came forward about her diagnosis of bipolar 2 disorder and published her blog, Halfway2Hannah where she discusses a range of mental health topics. Since then her blog has grown and most recently was named by Healthline as one of the Best Bipolar Disorder Blogs of 2019. She is best known for her quotes and videos featured on

Photo by Ofer Yakov

social media where she shares her unapologetic message about living with a mental illness in society. Hannah also works as a Creative Director and is currently living in California. She is a collector of vintage love letters, and loves bringing her family and friends together for uniquely themed gatherings and parties. Follow her on Instagram @hannahdblum.

Made in the USA
Columbia, SC
18 September 2020

21121847R00074